If lost, return to:

_____ .

_____

_____

_____

thanks.

ADVENTURE #1

WHERE WE WENT:

WHAT WE LEARNED::

WHO CAME:

WHAT WE DID:

FAVORITE PART::

NOTES :

_____

_____

ADVENTURE #2

WHERE WE WENT:

WHO CAME:

WHAT WE LEARNED::

WHAT WE DID:

FAVORITE PART::

NOTES :

_____

_____

ADVENTURE #3

WHERE WE WENT:

WHAT WE LEARNED::

WHO CAME:

WHAT WE DID:

FAVORITE PART::

NOTES :

ADVENTURE #4

WHERE WE WENT:

WHAT WE LEARNED::

WHO CAME:

WHAT WE DID:

FAVORITE PART::

NOTES :

_____

_____

ADVENTURE #5

WHERE WE WENT:

WHO CAME:

WHAT WE LEARNED::

WHAT WE DID:

FAVORITE PART::

NOTES :

ADVENTURE #6

WHERE WE WENT:

WHAT WE LEARNED::

WHO CAME:

WHAT WE DID:

FAVORITE PART::

NOTES :

_____

_____

ADVENTURE #7

WHERE WE WENT:

WHAT WE LEARNED::

WHO CAME:

WHAT WE DID:

FAVORITE PART::

NOTES :

ADVENTURE #8

WHERE WE WENT:

WHAT WE LEARNED::

WHO CAME:

WHAT WE DID:

FAVORITE PART::

NOTES :

_____

_____

ADVENTURE #9

WHERE WE WENT:

WHO CAME:

WHAT WE LEARNED::

WHAT WE DID:

FAVORITE PART::

NOTES :

ADVENTURE #10

WHERE WE WENT:

WHAT WE LEARNED::

WHO CAME:

WHAT WE DID:

FAVORITE PART::

NOTES :

_____

_____

ADVENTURE #11

WHERE WE WENT:

WHAT WE LEARNED::

WHO CAME:

WHAT WE DID:

FAVORITE PART::

NOTES :

ADVENTURE #12

WHERE WE WENT:

WHO CAME:

WHAT WE DID:

WHAT WE LEARNED::

FAVORITE PART::

NOTES :

_____

_____

ADVENTURE #13

WHERE WE WENT:

WHO CAME:

WHAT WE LEARNED::

WHAT WE DID:

FAVORITE PART::

NOTES :

ADVENTURE #14

WHERE WE WENT:

WHO CAME:

WHAT WE LEARNED::

WHAT WE DID:

FAVORITE PART::

NOTES :

ADVENTURE #15

WHERE WE WENT:

WHO CAME:

WHAT WE LEARNED::

WHAT WE DID:

FAVORITE PART::

NOTES :

ADVENTURE #16

WHERE WE WENT:

WHAT WE LEARNED::

WHO CAME:

WHAT WE DID:

FAVORITE PART::

NOTES :

_____

_____

ADVENTURE #17

WHERE WE WENT:

WHAT WE LEARNED::

WHO CAME:

WHAT WE DID:

FAVORITE PART::

NOTES :

_____

_____

ADVENTURE #18

WHERE WE WENT:

WHO CAME:

WHAT WE DID:

WHAT WE LEARNED::

FAVORITE PART::

NOTES :

ADVENTURE #19

WHERE WE WENT:

WHO CAME:

WHAT WE LEARNED::

WHAT WE DID:

FAVORITE PART::

NOTES :

_____

_____

ADVENTURE #20

WHERE WE WENT:

WHAT WE LEARNED::

WHO CAME:

WHAT WE DID:

FAVORITE PART::

NOTES :

_____

_____

ADVENTURE #21

WHERE WE WENT:

WHAT WE LEARNED::

WHO CAME:

WHAT WE DID:

FAVORITE PART::

NOTES :

_____

_____

ADVENTURE #22

WHERE WE WENT:

WHAT WE LEARNED::

WHO CAME:

WHAT WE DID:

FAVORITE PART::

NOTES :

ADVENTURE #23

WHERE WE WENT:

WHAT WE LEARNED::

WHO CAME:

WHAT WE DID:

FAVORITE PART::

NOTES :

ADVENTURE #24

WHERE WE WENT:

WHAT WE LEARNED::

WHO CAME:

WHAT WE DID:

FAVORITE PART::

NOTES :

_____

_____

ADVENTURE #25

WHERE WE WENT:

WHAT WE LEARNED::

WHO CAME:

WHAT WE DID:

FAVORITE PART::

NOTES :

ADVENTURE #26

WHERE WE WENT:

WHO CAME:

WHAT WE DID:

WHAT WE LEARNED::

FAVORITE PART::

NOTES :

ADVENTURE #27

WHERE WE WENT:

WHO CAME:

WHAT WE DID:

WHAT WE LEARNED::

FAVORITE PART::

NOTES :

_____

_____

ADVENTURE #28

WHERE WE WENT:

WHO CAME:

WHAT WE DID:

WHAT WE LEARNED::

FAVORITE PART::

NOTES :

ADVENTURE #29

WHERE WE WENT:

WHAT WE LEARNED::

WHO CAME:

WHAT WE DID:

FAVORITE PART::

NOTES :

_____

_____

ADVENTURE #30

WHERE WE WENT:

WHO CAME:

WHAT WE LEARNED::

WHAT WE DID:

FAVORITE PART::

NOTES :

_____

_____

ADVENTURE #31

WHERE WE WENT:

WHO CAME:

WHAT WE DID:

WHAT WE LEARNED::

FAVORITE PART::

NOTES :

ADVENTURE #32

WHERE WE WENT:

WHO CAME:

WHAT WE DID:

WHAT WE LEARNED::

FAVORITE PART::

NOTES :

_____

_____

ADVENTURE #33

WHERE WE WENT:

WHAT WE LEARNED::

WHO CAME:

WHAT WE DID:

FAVORITE PART::

NOTES :

ADVENTURE #34

WHERE WE WENT:

WHAT WE LEARNED::

WHO CAME:

WHAT WE DID:

FAVORITE PART::

NOTES :

_____

_____

ADVENTURE #35

WHERE WE WENT:

WHAT WE LEARNED::

WHO CAME:

WHAT WE DID:

FAVORITE PART::

NOTES :

_____

_____

ADVENTURE #36

WHERE WE WENT:

WHO CAME:

WHAT WE DID:

WHAT WE LEARNED::

FAVORITE PART::

NOTES :

_____

_____

ADVENTURE #37

WHERE WE WENT:

WHO CAME:

WHAT WE LEARNED::

WHAT WE DID:

FAVORITE PART::

NOTES :

_____

_____

ADVENTURE #38

WHERE WE WENT:

WHAT WE LEARNED::

WHO CAME:

WHAT WE DID:

FAVORITE PART::

NOTES :

ADVENTURE #39

WHERE WE WENT:

WHO CAME:

WHAT WE DID:

WHAT WE LEARNED::

FAVORITE PART::

NOTES :

_____

_____

ADVENTURE #40

WHERE WE WENT:

WHAT WE LEARNED::

WHO CAME:

WHAT WE DID:

FAVORITE PART::

NOTES :

ADVENTURE #41

WHERE WE WENT:

WHAT WE LEARNED::

WHO CAME:

WHAT WE DID:

FAVORITE PART::

NOTES :

_____

_____

ADVENTURE #42

WHERE WE WENT:

WHAT WE LEARNED::

WHO CAME:

WHAT WE DID:

FAVORITE PART::

NOTES :

ADVENTURE #43

WHERE WE WENT:

WHAT WE LEARNED::

WHO CAME:

WHAT WE DID:

FAVORITE PART::

NOTES :

_____

_____

ADVENTURE #44

WHERE WE WENT:

WHO CAME:

WHAT WE LEARNED::

WHAT WE DID:

FAVORITE PART::

NOTES :

_____

_____

ADVENTURE #45

WHERE WE WENT:

WHAT WE LEARNED::

WHO CAME:

WHAT WE DID:

FAVORITE PART::

NOTES :

ADVENTURE #46

WHERE WE WENT:

WHO CAME:

WHAT WE LEARNED::

WHAT WE DID:

FAVORITE PART::

NOTES :

ADVENTURE #47

WHERE WE WENT:

WHO CAME:

WHAT WE LEARNED::

WHAT WE DID:

FAVORITE PART::

NOTES :

ADVENTURE #48

WHERE WE WENT:

WHO CAME:

WHAT WE LEARNED::

WHAT WE DID:

FAVORITE PART::

NOTES :

_____

_____

ADVENTURE #49

WHERE WE WENT:

WHO CAME:

WHAT WE LEARNED::

WHAT WE DID:

FAVORITE PART::

NOTES :

_____

_____

ADVENTURE #50

WHERE WE WENT:

WHO CAME:

WHAT WE LEARNED::

WHAT WE DID:

FAVORITE PART::

NOTES :

Printed in Great Britain
by Amazon